T·H·E C·O·M·P·L·E·T·E
H·O·M·E
C·O·N·F·E·C·T·I·O·N·E·R

Hilary Walden

T·H·E C·O·M·P·L·E·T·E
H·O·M·E
C·O·N·F·E·C·T·I·O·N·E·R

Hilary Walden

In association with the
kitchen of Silver Spoon

Macdonald

A **Macdonald** BOOK

Copyright © 1986 Quarto Publishing Ltd

First published in Great Britain in 1987 by
Macdonald & Co (Publishers) Ltd
London & Sydney

A member of BPCC plc

British Library Cataloguing in Publication Data
Walden, Hilary
    The complete home confectioner.
    1. Candy
    I. Title
    641.8'53   TX791

    ISBN 0-356-13026-6

Filmset by Text Filmsetters Limited, Orpington, Kent

Manufactured in Hong Kong by Regent Publishing Services Limited
Printed in Hong Kong by Leefung Asco Printers Limited

Senior Editor Lorraine Dickey
Editors Tessa Rose and Sue Fleming
Art Editor Moira Clinch
Design Assistant Vincent Murphy

Photography Paul Forrester
Home Economist Philippa Caney

Art Director Alastair Campbell
Editorial Director Jim Miles

Equipment courtesy of David Mellor, 26 James Street, Covent Garden;
4 Sloane Square; 66 King Street, Manchester.
China courtesy of The General Store, Covent Garden.
Gas Hob courtesy of Wilec Ltd.
Border Illustration on pages 46, 47 designed by Collier Campbell.
Border Illustration on pages 52-53 designed by Ann Brecknell, Gordon
Fraser Gallery Ltd.

Macdonald & Co (Publishers) Ltd
Greater London House
Hampstead Road
London NW1 7QX

C·O·N·T·E·N·T·S

• SCISSORS •

Strong, sharp kitchen scissors are needed for cutting toffees and pulled sweets.

• METAL CUTTERS •

A selection of shapes and sizes of sharp metal cutters are required for marshmallows, fondants and marzipans.

• DIPPING FORKS •

Dipping forks can either have a loop at one end or two or three prongs. In addition to being used for dipping sweets they can be used to mark the surface with a pattern or design, but are not vital for either task; carving forks, fondue forks or ordinary kitchen forks can easily be used instead.

• FONDANT MAT •

A fondant mat is rather like a rubber ice-cube tray except that the indentations are a selection of decorative shapes. They can be used for shaping creams and chocolates as well as fondants.

• WRAPPING MATERIALS •

A number of materials can be used for wrapping sweets individually. The most straightforward is greaseproof paper but, for a more attractive presentation, clear cellophane or cling film can be used to show off the gloss and shiny colour of sweets to full effect. Aluminium foil and metallic wrapping paper, available in a wide range of colours from stationers and gift shops, can be very attractive. Alternatively, coloured cellophane can be used.

The wrapping for square or oblong sweets can either be folded over neatly to make a tidy parcel or it can simply be folded over the sweets and two opposite ends twisted in opposite directions. This method is most suitable for round sweets, humbugs or cushions.

Sweets that are not wrapped can be put in small plain paper sweet cases or into pretty decorated or foil ones. If two layers of sweets rather than a single one are packed inside a box, separate the layers with a sheet of greaseproof paper.

• STORAGE CONTAINERS AND STORING •

Unless sweets are to be eaten very soon after they have been made, they should be protected from the moisture in the atmosphere to prevent them becoming sticky. Some sweets such as caramels, toffees, boiled and 'pulled' sweets, must be wrapped individually before being placed in containers, while others, such as marshmallows, can simply be put carefully into a container that has first been lined with greaseproof paper.

Containers may be made of any material provided it is airtight and inert (with no smell that would taint the sweets). Glass jars allow the natural sparkle and colours of sweets or colourful wrappings to be displayed invitingly. If the jar does not have a suitable lid, cover it tightly with foil, cellophane or cling film, and secure it firmly with string or sticky tape.

Store all sweets in a cool, dry place. In general, the harder the sweet, the longer it will keep.

• A GUIDE TO STORAGE TIMES •

Simple sweets	Eat quickly as their perishable contents tend to dry out
Truffles	2-3 days
Chocolates	10-14 days
Jellies	2 weeks
Nutty Sweets	2 weeks
Candied and crystallized fruits	6 months
Fudge	3-4 weeks
Caramels	10-14 days
Marzipan, uncooked	1-2 days
Marzipan, unshaped but cooked	3-4 weeks
Marzipan sweets	Eat within 3 weeks
Boiled sweets	3-4 weeks
Nougat	3-4 weeks
Toffees	2 weeks
Fondant, uncooked	Use immediately
Fondant, boiled	6 months

I·N·G·R·E·D·I·E·N·T·S

The ingredients lists for most sweets are very short and simple, and all the important ingredients are in everyday use or readily available. Even the more specialist ingredients, such as concentrated food flavours or glucose, are not too difficult to obtain as they are stocked by good food shops or chemists.

• SUGAR •

Sugar is synonymous with sweets, and its many forms and states can be used to produce different types of sweets, with each type of sugar imparting different characteristics to the sweet.

Granulated. This is suitable for most recipes that are heated, but its large crystals will give a rather granular texture to uncooked confections.

Caster. This has finer crystals, therefore dissolves more readily. Thus it is more suitable than granulated for uncooked pastes.

Icing. This has a very fine texture so is ideal for uncooked sweets that must be very smooth. It is also sprinkled onto the work surface and rolling pin to prevent mixtures sticking when they are rolled out, and it is sprinkled into tins, when making marshmallows, for example.

Light soft brown. Fine grained with moist, clinging crystals that dissolve easily and impart a mild, yet distinctive flavour, this sugar is often used for fudge.

Dark soft brown. This sugar is richly flavoured and coloured, with moist, fine crystals that tend to clump together yet dissolve readily.

Demerara. This has a rich flavour with light golden crystals that remain separate but, as they are large, melt slowly. Because of this, it is best used in mixtures that are boiled to a high temperature, such as toffee.

Glucose. Available in both powder and liquid form, it is added to sweet mixtures to help control crystallization. It helps to keep sweets made from uncooked fondant soft for longer periods.

Honey. Added for the characteristic flavour it will impart, honey also helps to control crystallization.

Golden syrup. A British product that is a clear, pale, yellow-gold colour with a thick, honey-like consistency and mild flavour. Its inclusion in a recipe will help to control crystallization of the sugar.

Corn syrup. An American product with a mild flavour that, like honey and golden syrup, helps to keep the mixture smooth by controlling the formation of sugar crystals.

Black treacle. A thick, dark, richly-flavoured syrup that adds distinction to any sweet in which it is used.

Molasses. This has many similarities to black treacle but is less sweet.

• BUTTER •

Only use good quality unsalted butters, and dice them before use to speed up the melting.

• CHOCOLATE •

Special 'dipping' chocolate or good quality dessert chocolate are the best types to buy for making sweets; using cheap 'cooking' chocolate is a waste of your efforts and produces an inferior sweet. For that real rich flavour, use a bitter variety of plain chocolate.

• MILKS •

Evaporated and condensed milks give more richly flavoured sweets as they have been subjected to high temperatures for quite long periods during their processing, and so already have a caramel flavour.

• FLAVOURINGS •

So that they will not dilute the syrup, any flavourings that are added must be concentrated and sufficiently strong that only a few drops will be enough to flavour a thick sweet mixture. They are invariably added at the end of the cooking to avoid loss of strength through evaporation or breakdown of the constituents.

• COLOURINGS •

Pure vegetable food colourings are available from good grocers in a wide range of colours. Like flavourings, they are concentrated and used in small amounts either directly in the mixture or painted on to produce subtle shading and tints.

• INGREDIENTS•

1 Liquid glucose   7 Demerara sugar
2 Clear honey   8 Icing sugar
3 Golden syrup   9 Powdered glucose
4 Dark corn syrup   10 Granulated Sugar
5 Dark, soft brown sugar   11 Liquid food colourings
6 Light, soft brown sugar   12 Plain chocolate

A·L·L A·B·O·U·T S·U·G·A·R

Boiling sugar in water to make a syrup is the cornerstone of sweet making. And the degree to which the syrup is boiled, or the temperature that it reaches, will determine the type of sweet that is made. The more sugar there is in a syrup, or the less water, the higher the temperature of the boiling point of the solution. As the syrup continues to boil, more water evaporates, concentrating the syrup further and raising the boiling point. The greater the sugar content of a syrup, the firmer or harder it will set as it cools: for instance, the syrup for making toffees is taken to a higher temperature than that for making fudge, so the proportion of water is less, and the sweet harder.

During the heating the sugar is constantly changing. These changes are related to the temperature and concentration of the syrup, so it is very easy to tell what stage has been reached, either by measuring the temperature or carrying out a simple 'water test' (see page 18).

The initial proportions of water and sugar are not critical as it is the final concentration that matters, but obviously if too much water is added at the start it will take longer to evaporate off the excess and to reach the required temperature, so wasting time and fuel. As the temperature increases, so does the amount of sugar that water will 'take'.

When the syrup cools the sucrose in the sugar in such a syrup is very likely to re-form into crystals unless preventive steps are taken (see below, and individual recipes). But in some sweets this inclination of sugar to crystallize is put to good use – in a *controlled* way – as in the beating of fudges or fondants.

• ANTI-CRYSTALLIZING AGENTS •

Acids such as cream of tartar, lemon juice or vinegar break sucrose down into other sugars.

Sugars other than sucrose could be used, such as honey, liquid glucose or corn syrup.

Milks, cream and butter will thicken the syrup, and so hinder the formation of crystals.

• PREPARING A SUGAR SYRUP •

1 If a sugar thermometer is being used, place it in hot water.

2 Measure the sugar and liquid into a clean, thick, deep saucepan that has a capacity of about four times the volume of the ingredients.

3 Heat gently, stirring with a wooden spoon, until the sugar has dissolved.

4 Bring the syrup to the boil without stirring – this would cause crystals to form.

5 Cover the saucepan with a tight-fitting lid so that the steam that condenses on the sides of the pan will wash down any sugar that has crystallized there.

6 An alternative method of removing sugar crystals that form on the side of a saucepan is to use a clean brush dipped in hot water.

7 Remove the lid after about 3 minutes and put the warmed thermometer in position. Leave the syrup to boil until the correct temperature has been reached, adjusting the heat to maintain a steady boil.

If using a testing method (see page 18) rather than a thermometer to check the temperature of the syrup, carefully remove the pan from the heat and dip the bottom in cold water to arrest the temperature rise. Carry out the test. If the right stage has not been reached, return the pan to the heat and continue boiling.

8 As soon as the required temperature has been reached, remove the pan from the heat and dip the bottom in cold water.

• TESTING THE TEMPERATURE OF A SYRUP •

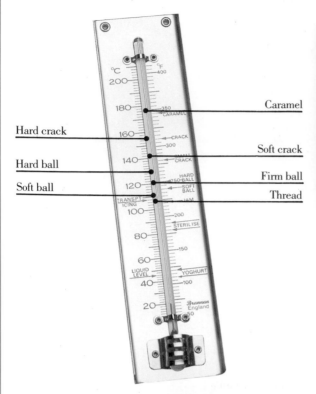

See page 14 for information on different types of sugar

Soft ball 112–116°C/234–240°F

Dip the pan in cold water. Drop a small amount of the syrup into a bowl of very cold water, roll it into a ball in the water, then lift it out.

If the syrup forms a ball whilst in the water but becomes soft and flattens under slight pressure when removed from the water, the correct stage has been reached.

Used for fondants and fudge.

Hard ball 121–130°C/250–266°F

Dip the pan in cold water. Drop a small amount of the syrup into very cold water, form it into a ball in the water, then lift it out.

If the ball holds its shape under slight pressure but is still quite sticky, the correct temperature has been reached.

Used for nougat and marshmallows.

Soft crack 132–143°C/270–290°F

Dip the pan in cold water. Drop a small amount of the syrup into very cold water. Remove it between the fingers then gently separate them.

If the syrup forms threads that are hard but not brittle the correct stage has been reached.

Used for humbugs.

Thread 106–113°C/223–236°F

Dip the pan in cold water. Using a teaspoon, take a small amount of the syrup then gently and slowly pour it over the rim of the spoon.

If a thin thread forms the correct temperature has been reached.

Firm ball 118–121°C/244–250°F

Dip the pan in cold water. Drop a small amount of the syrup into very cold water, roll it into a ball in the water, then lift it out.

If a ball holds its shape when lifted from the water but loses it as it warms up, the correct temperature has been reached.

Used for caramels.

Hard crack 149–154°C/300–310°F

Dip the pan in cold water. Drop a little of the syrup into very cold water, then remove it.

If it is hard and brittle the correct stage has been reached.

Used for hard toffee and rock.

Caramel 160–177°C/320–350°F

Dip the pan in cold water. Pour a small amount from a spoon onto a white plate. A golden honey indicates a light caramel, a golden amber colour a dark caramel. If the syrup darkens beyond this stage it will begin to taste bitter.

Used for pralines.

F·U·D·G·E

The sugar syrup for fudge is boiled to the soft ball stage and is then beaten to encourage crystallization of the sugar and give the fudge its characteristic texture and appearance. These can, in fact, be changed slightly by beating the syrup at different times—immediately after it has been cooked or after it has been left to cool. Firmer sweets with a more granular texture will result from beating in hot syrup whilst smooth fudge is the outcome of leaving the syrup to cool.

Stir fudge mixtures with a high milk or cream content to prevent them sticking and burning, and be sure to use a large enough saucepan as they will boil up considerably. (For a selection of fudge recipes, see pages 98-109.)

1 Place the thermometer in hot water to warm it. Oil the tin.

2 Gently heat the sugar with the milk, cream or diced butter and any other ingredients according to the recipe, in a thick saucepan that has a capacity at least four times the volume of the ingredients, stirring with a wooden spoon until the sugar has dissolved and any butter or chocolate melted.

3 Bring to the boil, cover and boil for about 3 minutes.

4 Uncover and boil until the required temperature has been reached, stirring as necessary if the mixture has a high milk or cream content.

5 Dip the pan in cold water.

6 Either beat the mixture immediately with a wooden spoon until it begins to thicken and becomes lighter in colour and loses its gloss, then quickly pour into the tin and leave until beginning to set. Or, leave the mixture to cool to about 50°C/122°F and starting to become opaque, then beat until it becomes paler and thickens (below).

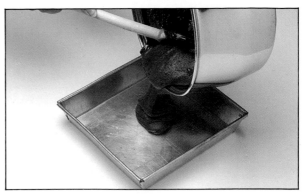

7 Pour into the tin and leave to set.

8 Mark into squares and leave to set completely.

9 Break into pieces and store in an airtight container between layers of greaseproof paper.

F·O·N·D·A·N·T

Fondant consists essentially of a mass of minute sugar crystals surrounded by a saturated sugar syrup. The creamy, smooth, melting texture is achieved through a series of precise stages, the first of which is the addition of glucose to the syrup to make sure that the sugar crystals formed during the later stages remain small so keeping the fondant smooth (glucose keeps the fondant softer for longer than would cream of tartar or another acid). The next stage is when the hot syrup is poured into a pool and the edges folded inwards to cool it quickly and evenly before it is 'worked' to develop the crystallization of the sugar. To free it of lumps the fondant is kneaded, like a dough for bread. It must then be left for at least 12 hours for the sugar crystals to undergo their final change, softening the fondant.

4 Using a dampened metal scraper or large metal palette knife, lift the edges of the pool of syrup and fold them to the centre. Repeat until the syrup becomes glossy and viscous and has a faint yellow colour. (below)

1 Sprinkle an even coating of cold water over a marble slab or other suitable work surface.
2 Prepare a sugar, incorporating glucose, to 116°C/240°F, the soft ball stage.

3 Dip the saucepan in cold water then quickly pour the syrup into a pool onto the surface and leave to cool for a few minutes.

5 Using a dampened wooden spatula work the mixture in a continuous figure of eight action for 5–10 minutes.

6 Stir until it becomes white and crumbly and the stirring is extremely difficult.

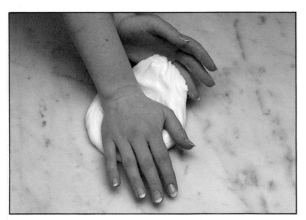

8 Form the fondant into a ball, place it on a dampened plate, cover with a damp cloth to prevent the surface drying out and leave in a cool place for at least 12 hours.

7 With lightly moistened hands, form a ball of fondant then knead it by pushing half of the ball away from you with the heel of one hand, fold the half back into the lump using a metal scraper or palette knife and repeat in a flowing action for 5–10 minutes until the mixture is free of lumps and feels smooth.

• FONDANT-DIPPED FRUITS •

1 Fruits that have a stem or stalk – hold the fruit by the stem or stalk then dip it into the melted fondant so that it is about three-quarters coated.

2 Lift it out, allowing the excess to drain off and dip in sugar.

3 Leave the fruit on waxed paper to dry.

4 Portions of fruit without stems – place the fruit on a dipping fork and lower it into the melted fondant. Turn it over so that it is completely coated.

5 Lift the fruit out on the dipping fork, tap the fork lightly on the side of the bowl then draw the bottom of the fork across the edge of the bowl. Carefully transfer the fruit to waxed paper and leave to dry.

C·A·R·A·M·E·L·S

The traditional mellow, soft, creamy flavour of caramel sweets is obtained by the addition of milk, or milk products such as cream, evaporated or condensed milk, and butter, and not, as the name suggests, by caramelizing the sugar. The characteristic chewy, moist texture comes from boiling the syrup as far as the firm ball stage, 118–121°C/244–250°F. However, the degree of firmness can be varied by taking the syrup to different points within the firm-hard ball range – the nearer to the top of the range, the firmer the sweet.

It is especially important when making caramels to use a sufficiently large saucepan because the mixture expands considerably as it boils. Because of their milk, cream or butter content, caramels are liable to stick to the saucepan and therefore burn, so stirring becomes a necessity. Their thickening effect on the syrup provides some protection against crystallization of the sugar, but for a complete safeguard another anti-crystallizing agent (see page 18) is usually added as well. (A selection of caramel recipes may be found on pages 110-15.)

2 Gently heat the sugar with the milk, cream or diced butter and anti-crystallizing agent in a heavy saucepan that has a capacity at least four times the volume of the ingredients.

1 Line the base of a tin with a piece of oiled greaseproof paper.

3 Stir with a wooden spoon until the sugar has dissolved and any butter melted.

4 Bring to the boil, cover and boil for about 3 minutes.

5 Put the warmed thermometer in place and boil, stirring gently occasionally and taking care not to knock the thermometer, until the syrup reaches the required temperature.

6 Dip the saucepan in cold water to prevent the temperature rising further, then pour the caramel into the tin.

7 Leave to cool. Mark it into pieces when just beginning to set and before it becomes too hard. Oiling the knife will prevent sticking.

8 When the caramel is completely cold and firm, turn it out of the tin, remove the paper and divide it into the marked pieces. Wrap the caramel pieces in cellophane or greaseproof paper.

M·A·R·S·H·M·A·L·L·O·W·S

The basis for marshmallows is a syrup boiled to the hard ball stage, 121–130°C/250–266°F. Gelatine and stiffly beaten egg white are incorporated to transform it into softly set airy clouds.

The syrup with the dissolved gelatine must be poured into the egg whites in a slow, thin, steady stream, and the whites must be whisked constantly otherwise the weight of the syrup will knock the air bubbles out of them. A food mixer is therefore a great boon, but failing that, place the bowl containing the egg whites on a damp cloth to hold it steady. Whisking must continue until the mixture is very fluffy and light before it can be left to set. For this, an oiled tin well dusted with a mixture of sifted cornflour and icing sugar is used. All the surfaces of marshmallows are coated in cornflour/icing sugar to prevent them sticking together. (See page 82 for Marshmallows recipes.)

1 Prepare the tin.

2 Boil a syrup to the hard ball stage.

3 Meanwhile, mix the gelatine with a little cold water in a small bowl, place the bowl in a larger bowl of hot water and heat until dissolved.

4 Whisk the egg whites with a wire whisk (this gives a greater volume than a rotary or electric whisk) until stiff peaks are formed.

5 Add the gelatine to the syrup.

6 Then pour the syrup into the egg whites in a slow, thin, steady stream down the sides of the bowl.

7 Continue to whisk the mixture until it is very fluffy and light and just holds its shape firmly but is still thin enough to turn into the tin without difficulty. This may take 15–20 minutes.

8 Turn the mixture into the tin, lightly smoothing it out evenly and levelling the surface with a metal palette knife. Leave to set.

9 Sift an even coating of cornflour mixed with icing sugar onto the work surface. Loosen around the sides of the tin containing the marshmallow with a small knife then invert the marshmallow onto the prepared surface.

10 Lightly coat the top and sides with cornflour/ icing sugar. Cut into pieces using a large, oiled knife or sharp scissors or oiled metal cutters.

11 Coat the sides of the pieces with cornflour/icing sugar, then place on a wire rack to dry.

'P·U·L·L·E·D' S·W·E·E·T·S

The technique of 'pulling' is used to produce humbugs, rock and taffies. It involves forming syrup that has been boiled to 130–143°C/266–290°F, the hottest hard ball to soft crack stage, into a sausage shape, after it has been cooled slightly, then repeatedly pulling, folding and twisting it to incorporate a mass of tiny air bubbles, and give a shiny, silvery appearance. It requires strength and stamina – and hands that can withstand high temperatures as it is essential to work the syrup whilst it is as hot as possible because it looses pliability as it cools.

---

1 Prepare the syrup to the required temperature and oil a marble slab or other suitable surface.

2 Dip the saucepan in cold water then pour the syrup quickly into a pool on the surface. Leave it to cool briefly until a light skin forms on the surface.

3 Using an oiled metal scraper or large metal palette knife, lift the edges of the pool of syrup and fold them into the centre. Repeat until the syrup is just cool enough to handle.

4 With oiled hands, to prevent sticking, and the scraper or palette knife, form the syrup into a sausage shape. Lift it up with your hands and pull it out to about 45 cm/18 in. Fold it back together and repeat the pulling and folding until the syrup changes from being soft and slightly sticky to a firmer, more shiny texture. Fold the pulled syrup in half, twist the two strands together then pull the twisted sausage out until it is about 1 cm/½ in in diameter. Repeat the folding, twisting and pulling until it becomes opaque, shiny, and is no longer pliable. This may take up to 20 minutes.

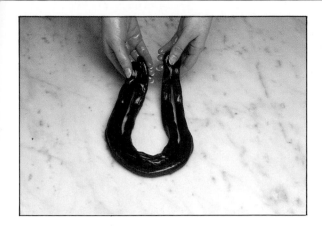

6 Using strong oiled scissors cut across the rope to form cushion shapes.

7 Wrap the sweets in cellophane or greaseproof paper and store in an airtight container.

• DUAL-COLOURED BOILED SWEETS •

The 'pulling' technique can also be used to make dual-coloured boiled sweets. They can either be made by combining 'ropes' of two different coloured syrups, one pulled until it is opaque and pearlized, the other left shiny and translucent; or by dividing a syrup in half and pulling one half until it is pale but leaving the other half shiny then twisting the two together.

1 Oil a work surface.

2 Prepare a syrup using a brown sugar.

3 Pour the syrup into two pools onto the surface. As the edges of the pools begin to cool slightly, lift them and fold them into the centre using an oiled metal scraper or large metal palette knife.

4 With oiled hands, form one pool into a sausage shape, then pull, fold and twist it as in step 4 on page 30.

5 With oiled hands form the second pool into a sausage then pull it to form a similar length to the first, without working it so that its colour hardly changes.

6 Lay the two pieces side by side, twist them together, then fold the length that is formed over and over to make a short rope.

7 Gently but firmly and quickly and giving a twist, pull along the length of the rope to produce a long, thin, twisted, even strand.

8 Using lightly oiled scissors cut into pieces giving the rope a half turn towards you so the pieces have triangular surfaces.

9 Store in an airtight container between layers of greaseproof paper.

5 Fold the stretched-out sausage in half then in half again and gently twist the four strands together. Pull out again, gently twisting.

4 After trimming the edges of the rectangle with a sharp knife, cut it lengthways into 3 strips of equal width.

5 Brush the top of one strip lightly with lightly beaten egg white.

6 Place another strip on top, making sure that it is completely lined up. Repeat with the remaining strip.

7 Cut the stack lengthways into 4 strips with a long, sharp knife.

8 Lay one strip flat and place a second strip on the first, turning it over so the colours are reversed. Brush with egg white and repeat with the remaining strips, making sure the colours always alternate.

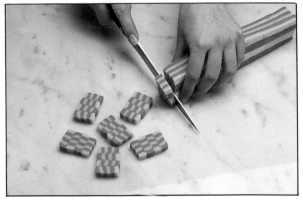

9 Cut into slices using a sharp knife then leave to dry on greaseproof paper for a few hours.

C·O·N·T·A·I·N·E·R·S A·N·D W·R·A·P·P·I·N·G·S

Homemade sweets do not need to have any adornment – however, pretty or inventive packaging or wrapping can enhance the sense of occasion and 'specialness'.

• GLASS JARS•

Clear glass jars with ground glass or even screw-top closures are ideal for showing off sweets that do not crush easily.

If giving the sweets as a present tie a ribbon and bow around the neck of the jar and decorate the body of the jar with cut-out shapes of coloured paper. ▶

•INDIVIDUALLY• WRAPPED SWEETS

Sweets can be wrapped individually in clear cellophane that will allow the colour and sparkle of the sweet to show through, or a coloured cellophane, perhaps with an inner covering of foil, can be used. Plain thin aluminium foil, or coloured or decorated foils make very bright and attractive wrappings.

▼

•GIFT BOXES AND• ENVELOPES

A wide variety of boxes and other containers can be bought from good stationers.

If the sweets are likely to be crushed or squashed easily separate the layers of sweets with a sheet of card or corrugated paper.

For that extra special touch compose a matching set.

•LACY CONES•

▲ *Cones to hold sweets can also be made from decorative doilies. Very lacy white ones can look particularly effective if lined with plain material, but gold or silver ones can be left unlined. Simply form the doily into a cone shape and secure in place with staples. Thread a coloured ribbon through the top row of holes.*

•CERAMIC DISHES•

◀ *There is an extensive range of attractive ceramic dishes available which are very popular as gifts. One that can be filled with home-made sweets will give the present a personal touch. A genuine large shell could also be used.*

•BASKETS AND OTHER• CONTAINERS

Wicker bread baskets or small sewing baskets can be padded and lined with pretty paper and material (this could be trimmed with ribbon or broderie anglaise), encased in clear cellophane and finished with a bow.

Other useful containers include shallow foil dishes, disposable plastic and polystyrene pots and trays used for dairy products and vegetables. Cover with paper or material, add some decorative adhesive shapes and finish with bows (the ready-tied adhesive ones are handy) and ribbons.
▼

•CONES•

Cut out equal sized squares of greaseproof and decorative paper. Place the coloured paper with the pattern side down and cover with the greaseproof. Form into a cone by holding two opposite corners and rolling them together towards you. Secure the corners with coloured
◀ *staples or glue.*

•TOYS•

A container that is fun to play with after the sweets are eaten makes a good present
▲ *for children.*

C·H·R·I·S·T·M·A·S G·I·F·T·S

Christmas present giving can be notoriously difficult with many hours spent thinking and searching for just the right present. Yet with homemade sweets it is so easy to hit upon an ideal gift every time, whether it is just a small token or, something very special.

•CARTONS AND BOXES•

◀ *At Christmas time it is possible to buy all manner of pretty, decorated gift cartons and boxes and what better gift to fill them with than homemade sweets.*
Homemade Christmas

boxes can be made from any box over-wrapped with Christmas paper or, from a strip and disc of card stuck together and covered with Christmas paper.

•WINE GLASSES•

A more sophisticated Christmas stocking – from an everyday wine glass right through to expensive crystal. Cocktail or liqueur chocolates and truffles seem the obvious choice for filling the glass. Decorate with a bow and a sprig of holly. ▶

•CHRISTMAS STOCKING•

A selection of wrapped sweets makes an ideal stocking filler for children of all ages.
▼

•TABLE OR TRAY• DECORATIONS

Make attractive table or tray decorations with edible centres of soft pale green fondant rolled in chopped nuts. The leaves and flowers are made from coloured sweet cases. ▲

•DECORATED SWEETS•

Boxes of homemade sweets can be decorated with coloured marzipan or fondant.
▼

• MUGS AND DISHES•
A filling of homemade sweets adds a personal touch to bought mugs and ceramic dishes. ▶

• SHAPED SWEETS•
Marzipan and fondant can be coloured and flavoured, if liked, then formed into Christmasy shapes such as Christmas trees and stars to decorate cake or pudding plates. ▼

•CHRISTMAS CRACKERS•
Crackers are easy to make at home. Cut out equal sized rectangles of greaseproof and coloured cellophane, crepe, or decorative paper. Place the coloured paper, pattern side down, with the greaseproof on top. Cut out a piece of card, the same width as the paper but only ⅓ of the length. Place across the greaseproof paper. Form into a roll with the card inside. Twist one end about 5cm/2in from the end and fill the tube with sweets. Twist the other end. Decorate with ribbons, bows and decorative cut-out shapes. ▶

•SWEET BAGS•
Cut circles about 15cm/6in in diameter, depending on the number of sweets and their size, from crepe, tissue, cellophane paper or pretty fabric. If the sweets are not wrapped cut a lining of greaseproof or waxed paper for material bags. Trim the edge of the fabric with lace for an attractive finish. Place the sweets in the centre of the circle and gather up the paper or material over them. Tie with a ribbon and finish with a bow. ◀

•HANGING SWEETS•
Individually wrapped sweets can be tied with bows and ribbons to make decorations for the tree or elsewhere around the house. ▶

As it is well-known that in giving food we are fulfilling a basic desire to please those we love and care about, then to offer a gift that is indulgent, irresistible and personally made must be the most sincere and meaningful token of affection.

•CAR•

Presents that show a degree of fondness or caring, yet are not too overt, can be the most difficult to choose. A perfect solution is a gift that matches the person's hobby or interest, such as a car plus some homemade sweets all tied up with a simple bow of ribbon decorated with hearts.
▼

•BOXES•

Ordinary square and rectangular boxes with heart shapes on them can be bought but it is also easy to create the same effect yourself. Either cover a plain box with paper that has a heart design printed on it or, stick cut-out heart shapes on a plain box. A tin can also be covered or decorated in the same way.
▶

•HEART-SHAPED• BOXES

Heart-shaped boxes are available from most stationers. Fill with homemade sweets and add a red rose.
▶

•HEART-SHAPED• SWEETS

Actions speak louder than words and a box of heart-shaped homemade sweets says so much so simply. Or,

the message can be 'spelt out' by decorating the sweets in appropriate letters formed from marzipan or fondant or piped chocolate.
▼

LARGE HEART-
• SHAPED CONTAINER •

A large heart-shaped container can be made from a heart-shaped cake tin, placed on a base of stiff cardboard, cut to shape and then covered with red satin, crepe paper or foil. The bottom of the container can be padded with tissue paper. Liqueur or spirit-flavoured fondant chocolates finished with crystallised flowers or, luscious truffles are the most suitable sweets for such a lavish present. Add a bow of red ribbon and wrap the container and sweets in clear cellophane.

Small heart-shaped containers can be made in the same way using heart-shaped biscuit cutters. The sweets can be 'tied in' with ribbon crossed over them and tied ◀ into a big bow.

• SUSPENDED SWEET •
BAGS

For a glamorous 'fun' gift form small sweet bags from gold net, perhaps one that has a heart-shaped decoration on it. Decorate the filled bag with a small heart-shaped brooch and tie it up with ribbon decorated with hearts. ▶

• CERAMIC DISHES •
Search for heart-shaped ornamental dishes for pastel-coloured fondant sweets. Or, for a gift that is also functional – ideal for the enthusiastic cook – use

▲

heart-shaped white cœur à la crème moulds, available from kitchen-ware shops and departments of large stores.

E·A·S·T·E·R G·I·F·T·S

Easter is a bright, cheery time, a time for giving and for enjoying yourself. And what better way to capture the air of enthusiasm and generosity than with batches of homemade sweets.

• MUGS •

◄ *Combine a useful present with one that is delicious to eat. Pack fine strips of coloured cellophane paper in the bottom of the mug to form a 'nest' and over-wrap sweets that are piled up with cellophane paper to hold them in place.*

• DAFFODIL SWEETS •

Give an Easter air to chocolates, fondants or marzipans by decorating them with small crystallized primroses or small seasonal flowers, such as daffodils or narcissi formed out of coloured marzipan or fondant. ►

• CERAMIC DISHES •

Easter is associated with bright yellows, fresh greens, lambs and daffodils, so for an Easter present select a dish suitably coloured and decorated. ►

• EGG CUPS •

In the months approaching Easter, egg cups and similar small ceramic dishes shaped with chicks or small rabbits become available in the shops. These are ideal for filling with chocolate eggs or other homemade sweets.
▼

• DECORATING EASTER • EGGS

Easter eggs can be made to look as good as they taste in many ways. They can be wrapped in decorated foil; crystallized flowers or flowers formed out of fondant or marzipan can be 'stuck' onto the surface using a little melted chocolate; a design can be piped onto the surface or around the seam; or the egg can simply be tied in a pretty bow.

•CHRISTENING•

Easter is a popular time for christenings. For a gratifying yet lasting present give a porcelain ornament plus some homemade sweets. ▶

•EASTER SHAPES•

Chicks can be made from marzipan, coloured yellow, with the beaks moulded out of orange marzipan. Coloured feathers can be inserted to act as tails, with legs and feet made from coated wire.

Small rabbits can also be formed from coloured marzipan. Their tails can be made from cotton wool or make-up removing balls.

Easter eggs can, of course,

be made from moulded chocolate. They can also be formed from coloured marzipan or fondant, or even from chocolate truffle mixtures. Give a box filled with a selection of eggs.

•EGG TRAY•

A cardboard egg tray provides an obvious seasonal container for small Easter eggs nestling on a bed of 'straw' made out of fine strands of tissue paper. Do not forget to over-wrap the tray and eggs with cellophane paper. Smaller gifts can be made in the same way using the bottom portion of small size egg boxes. ▼

•CHOCOLATE RABBIT•

◀ Moulds are available for making chocolate rabbits in the same way as Easter eggs. Buy a small mould as well as a large one to make a family of rabbits.

Finish the rabbit with a ribbon tied in a bow around the neck.

• ABOVE •
Soft Cream Molasses Toffee
• OPPOSITE •
Brazil Nut Toffee Cushions

H·A·Z·E·L·N·U·T T·O·F·F·E·E

MAKES ABOUT 550 g/1¼ lb
·
75 g/3 oz shelled hazelnuts, roughly chopped
·
225 g/8 oz sugar
·
225 g/8 oz soft light brown sugar
·
40 g/1½ oz unsalted butter, diced
·
10 ml/2 teaspoons vinegar
·
A few drops of vanilla essence

1 Oil a tin approximately 17.5 cm/7 in square.
2 Spread the nuts out on a baking tray and warm gently in a very low oven.
3 Gently heat the sugars, butter and vinegar in 150 ml/¼ pt water in a heavy saucepan, stirring with a wooden spoon, until the sugars have dissolved and the butter melted.
4 Bring to the boil, cover and boil for 3 minutes.
5 Uncover and boil until the temperature reaches 149°C/300°F, the hard crack stage.

6 Add vanilla essence and pour half into the tin.
7 Scatter the nuts over the surface, then pour the remaining toffee over.
8 Leave until just beginning to set then mark into squares with a lightly oiled knife. Leave to set completely.
9 Break into squares and store in an airtight container wrapped individually in cellophane paper.

E·V·E·R·T·O·N T·O·F·F·E·E

MAKES ABOUT 750 g/1¾ lb
·
100 g/4 oz butter, chopped
·
350 g/12 oz demerara sugar
·
200 g/7 oz black treacle
·
150 g/5 oz golden syrup

1 Oil a tin approximately 20 cm/8 in square.
2 Gently heat the butter, sugar, black treacle and syrup in a heavy saucepan until the sugar has dissolved and the treacle melted, stirring with a wooden spoon.
3 Bring to the boil, cover and boil for 3 minutes.
4 Uncover and boil until the temperature reaches 143°C/290°F, the soft crack stage.
5 Plunge the bottom of the saucepan in cold water immediately.
6 Pour the toffee into the tin and leave until beginning to set.
7 Mark the toffee into squares using a lightly oiled knife and leave to set completely.
8 Break or cut into squares and store in an airtight container, wrapped individually in cellophane paper.

• ABOVE •
Hazelnut Toffee
• OPPOSITE •
Everton Toffee

F·O·N·D·A·N·T

Meltingly smooth 'creamy' fondant is extremely versatile. It can be flavoured in innumerable ways during its preparation or small amounts can be flavoured separately. It also has many uses, as it can be rolled out and cut into shapes, coated in chocolate, melted and poured into moulds, or used as a coating. As true fondant requires some expertise, inexperienced cooks will find the uncooked fondant more useful. (For illustrations of methods, see page 22.)

F·O·N·D·A·N·T
(uncooked)

MAKES ABOUT 450 g/1 lb
•
450 g/1 lb icing sugar, sieved
•
45 ml/3 tablespoons liquid glucose
•
1 egg white, lightly whisked
•
Flavouring and colouring (optional)

1 Lightly dust a work surface with extra icing sugar.
2 Mix the icing sugar and glucose together and add sufficient egg white to give a stiff but pliable mixture.
3 Turn onto the surface and knead very well until smooth and feeling slightly moist.
4 Form the fondant into a ball then flatten it out using a rolling pin.
5 Make a series of slits across the surface and put the flavouring and colouring into the slits.
6 Knead the fondant again to distribute the ingredients evenly.

7 Use as required, but remember that fondant does not keep and should be used immediately.

• ORANGE CREAMS •
Add a few drops of orange oil and orange food colouring.
1 Shape into small balls, then rub them lightly on a fine grater so the surface resembles orange peel.
2 Place a very small piece of angelica on the top of each to resemble the stalk.
3 Leave in a cool place for 24 hours to dry.

• PISTACHIO CREAMS •
Add a few drops of green food colouring.
1 Form into small balls then roll each ball in finely chopped pistachio nuts.

C·R·E·A·M
F·O·N·D·A·N·T
(uncooked)

MAKES ABOUT 450 g/1 lb
•
450 g/1 lb icing sugar
•
2.5 ml/1/2 teaspoon cream of tartar
•
45 ml/3 tablespoons double cream, whipped
•
1 small egg white, lightly whisked

1 Dust a work surface with extra sieved icing sugar.
2 Sieve the icing sugar and cream of tartar together.
3 Mix in the cream and sufficient whisked egg white to give a firm but pliable mixture.
4 Knead for 5 minutes on the work surface.
5 Roll out with a rolling pin dusted with icing sugar to about 1.5–2 cm/1/2–3/4 in thick and cut into shapes with a cutter lightly coated with icing sugar.

• ABOVE •
Uncooked Cream Fondant
• OPPOSITE •
Pistachio and Orange Creams

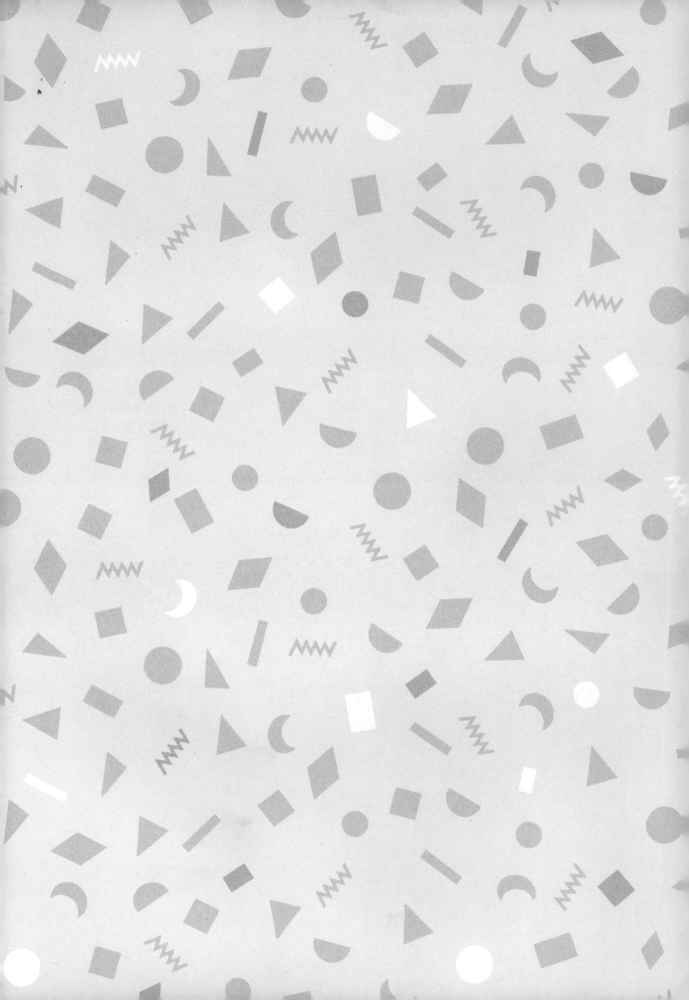

1

God Is the Creator

Your hands made us all.
ISAIAH 64:8

God made the tall giraffes and the tiny bumblebees. He made the mighty lions and the scaly fish. God directs the wind, and He tells the snowflakes where to fall. God is so creative, and He made us to be creative too! He gave us an imagination so we can create amazing things just as He did!

Creation

1 Day one the earth was dark as night;
Then God proclaimed, "Let there be light!"

2 Day two the sky was painted blue;
God made it brighter just for you.

3 Day three God split the land and sea,
Then made the plants and every tree!

4 Day four He made the moon and sun;
Across the sky the stars were strung.

5 Day five the oceans filled with fish,
And God made birds with wings to *swish*!

6 Day six the animals came to be—
Then God created you and me!

7 Day seven God said, "Now I'll rest,
For all I've made is good and blessed!"

The story of **creation** is found in Genesis 1–2.

The Shepherd Creates

I see the moon and stars,
which you created.

PSALM 8:3

God made the sun and moon,
The silly, snoopy, smart raccoon.

The star-filled skies, the mountaintop,
The oceans blue, the frogs that hop!

The puppy dogs to love and cuddle;
Drops of rain that splash and puddle.

The Shepherd made us ALL with care—
We see His glory *everywhere*!

Dear God, thank You for **showing** Your love in everything You've made.

Dear God, thank You for
being faithful to Your promises.

Bedtime Treasure

God has never broken a promise, and He never will.

Why should we keep our promises?

Dear God, help me to keep
my promises too. Amen.

4

You Can Talk to God

Never stop praying.
1 THESSALONIANS 5:17

Praying to God is simple. You can talk to Him like a friend! Just tell Him about your worries, and He can make you feel better. Thank Him for the good things He has given you, and tell God why you love Him. The great thing about prayer is that you can talk to God any time of the day! He will always hear you when you talk to Him, no matter what.

You Are Always Heard

I love the Lord because he
listens to my prayers.

PSALM 116:1

Close your eyes,
Fold your hands,
And whisper a prayer.

Open them up;
Put your hands in the air!

God always listens,
Whenever you call,

No matter which
words you use,
Fancy or small.

I know You hear me from the start.
I pray to You with all my **heart**.

Pray Every Day

Pray for your family,
Your neighbors and friends!
Ask God to bless them.
His love never ends!

GOD'S WORD

The Lord listens when I pray to him.

PSALM 4:3

Did you say a **prayer** to start your day?
Did you ask God to show you the way?

Bedtime Treasure

God loves to hear our prayers.

What do you like to talk to God about?

Dear God, thank You for
hearing my prayers! Amen.

5

God Blesses You

"May the Lord bless you and keep you."
NUMBERS 6:24

Blessings are the good things God has given to you. God gives us so many things to enjoy. He gave us furry animals, shade under the trees, beautiful skies, and loving family members and friends. God wants to give us blessings because He loves us. Giving us good things makes Him very happy.

Abraham

Abram was a **friend** of God.
He listened and obeyed.
He **honored** God both day and night,
And faithfully, he prayed.

He looked up at the **starlit** sky,
For God had told him to.
"You'll bring great **blessing** to the world
By what I'll do through you."

Abram became **Abraham**:
A father of the nations.
Our God is **true** in all His ways,
And that's our celebration!

The story of **Abraham** begins in Genesis 12.

The Shepherd Blesses

The Lord will bless those who fear him, from the smallest to the greatest.

PSALM 115:13

 What is a blessing? What is it like?
Is it a puppy, a flower, a bike?

A blessing is something that brings you joy.
It *might* be a pet, and it *could* be a toy.

A blessing is something good for you,
And often it will teach you too.

The Shepherd will send them, bundled with care.
Just look! His blessings are *everywhere*!

Dear God, thank You for putting

Your blessings all around me.

Dear God, thank You for blessing my life with smiles and grace.

Bedtime Treasure

God is so joyful when He thinks about His creation.

What made you happy this week?

Dear God, thank You for celebrating
when You think of me! Amen.

7

God Protects You

The Lord guards you. The Lord protects you as the shade protects you from the sun.
PSALM 121:5

God loves you very much and wants to protect you. He is like a shepherd who watches over His sheep day and night. God is never too busy or too tired to care for you. He will always be there. Even when something bad happens, God can protect you and turn that bad thing into something good!

Joseph

Joseph's coat—**colorful**, bright—
Helped to put him in a plight.

Jealous **brothers**, evil plan,
In a well it all began.

Egypt! Slavery! Jail! Dream!
God undid their **awful** scheme.

Joseph ruled the kingdom's grain;
Forgave his brothers in his reign.

Brave, godly, **humble**, and free,
Second in command was he!

Joseph's story begins in Genesis 37.

You Are Protected

God Most High protects me like a shield.

PSALM 7:10

Inside, outside,
All around,

In the country,
In the town.

God protects you
Every day

In every single
Sort of way!

I pray for protection—I know You are near.

God, bless me with **courage** to trust and not fear.

9

God Has a Plan for You

When a man's steps follow the Lord,
God is pleased with his ways.

PSALM 37:23

Did you know that God has a plan for you? God
wants the world to be full of His love, and He wants
us to help show His love to others! Sometimes this
may seem scary, but God will show us what to do.

Moses

Moses went to Pharaoh's court.
God sent him there, you see.
His people, Israel, needed help.
God planned to set them free.

Moses shouted, "Let them go!
Or God will judge this place.
Frogs and flies and death and cries—
These plagues you soon will face!"

Pharaoh said, "They cannot go!"
So bad things came to be,
Until he said, "Get out! Be gone!". . .
God's might had set them free!

The story of Moses and
Pharaoh begins in Exodus 5.

The Shepherd Guides

I praise the Lord because he guides me. Even at night, I feel his leading.

PSALM 16:7

The Shepherd goes ahead of you,
To guide you with His love.

He helps you when you ask Him to,
With wisdom from above.

And when you say your prayers at night,
He's listening—it's true!

He whispers to your little heart,
"I am taking care of you."

Dear God, thank You for

showing me just what to do!

The Ten Commandments are from Exodus 20.

The Shepherd Teaches

Those who obey what they
have been taught are happy.

PROVERBS 29:18

Learn what is good and right and true.
Do what the Shepherd teaches you.

Love God more than any other.
Listen close to father and mother!

Love your neighbor, be polite,
Trust the truth, and shine your light.

Keep your heart from staying mad,
And let your tears out when you're sad.

Lift your hope up to the sky—
And let your cares go flying by!

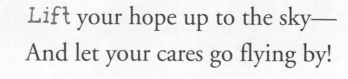

Dear God, thank You for **teaching** me what is true and good.

Bedtime Treasure

When we obey God, we make Him happy.

What does God want you to do?

Dear God, thank You for showing
me right from wrong. Amen.

The story of **David** and **Goliath**
is from 1 Samuel 17.

You Don't Have to Be Afraid

I trust in God. I will not be afraid.
PSALM 56:11

No matter what comes your way,
big things or small,

Say a prayer, trust in God,
and then stand up tall.

You can face anything—
God's on your side.

Put on your courage,
and don't ever hide!

I pray I will **trust** You and face all my fear.
You will help me and always be near.

Being faithful to God means
doing what He wants us to do.

What is something God wants you to do?
Have you ever been afraid to obey God?

Dear God, help me to be faithful
to You every day. Amen.

14

You Are Unique

God has made us what we are.
EPHESIANS 2:10

Did you know that there is no one on earth quite like you? You are one of a kind! Before you were born, God had a plan to make you unique. He gave you a special smile and a wonderful laugh. No one is exactly like you, and you are very important. God loves you just the way you are!

The Shepherd Chooses

"I chose you. Before you were born, I set you apart for a special work."

JEREMIAH 1:5

You are **one of a kind!**
In the world you won't find
Another someone like you.

You can search high and low,
Go beyond a **rainbow**,
But there's no one who smiles like you.

It is simple, you see;
You are different than me.
We're **unique** in our own sort of way.

The Shepherd **chose** you.
You have something to do—
And He'll guide you along every day.

Dear God, thank You for choosing me
to do something special in this world.

Good Night, God

Thank You for loving and
giving so generously!

Bedtime Treasure

Every good thing comes from God.

What has God given to you?

Dear God, thank You for all the gifts
You have given to me. Amen.

17

God Guides You

Lord, tell me your ways. Show me how
to live. Guide me in your truth.
PSALM 25:4–5

Have you ever walked into the wrong room? You
may have wanted to get a snack from the kitchen,
but you accidentally walked into your bedroom
instead. Everybody goes the wrong way sometimes.
But if we ever go the wrong way in life, like
when we disobey, God will guide us back to the
right path.

Jonah

God gave Jonah orders,
But he ran to the sea.
A big fish swallowed him right up
Because he chose to flee.

Three days in its belly,
Then God said, "Spit him out!
Nineveh must hear the words
I told Jonah to shout!"

Jonah tried to run away
But landed in the sea.
The lesson, here, is do not fear;
When God says, "Go"—agree!

The story of Jonah is from the book of Jonah.

The Shepherd Plans

The Lord's plans will
stand forever.

PSALM 33:11

A plan, a purpose, a path for you;
The Shepherd has something for you to do.

It may keep you near or lead you afar—
God's plan for you is as special as you are.

If you make a wrong turn and lose your way,
He'll guide you back; just stop and pray.

Dear God, thank You for making me part of Your *plan*.

19

Jesus Is God's Son

The Good News is about God's
Son, Jesus Christ our Lord.
ROMANS 1:3

Do you know who Jesus is? He is the perfect Son of God! He came to earth as a baby, and as He grew up, He taught people about God. Jesus loves everyone, and He teaches us how to love one another too. This is good news! We can be kind, good, and giving just like Jesus is!

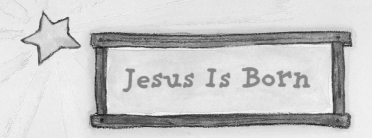

Jesus Is Born

Miracles happen! They do, they do!
The greatest miracle happened for you!

The Virgin Mary had God's Son.
The angels heralded, "He's the One!"

The shepherds came, the wise men too,
To see the King, who'd make us new.

A star, so bright, lit up the night;
The manger filled with heaven's light.

Baby Jesus, God's gift to all,
Was born to save both great and small.

Read more about the **birth** of Jesus
in Luke 2 and Matthew 2.

You Have a Loving Shepherd

The Lord is my shepherd.
I have everything I need.

PSALM 23:1

To guide you, to **lead** you,
To show you the way,

To love you, to see you,
To **help** you today,

To watch you, to **save** you,
To hear when you pray . . .

Jesus, your **Shepherd**,
Is with you to stay!

pray I will **follow** the way that You lead.

I thank You for giving me all that I need.

I pray You will teach me—I'll **listen** each day.

I trust You will help me to follow Your way.

The Shepherd watches

The LORD keeps watch over you as you come and go, both now and forever.

PSALM 121:8 NLT

I come and I go.
I'm fast and I'm slow.
But I'm never, ever alone.

I run and I play.
I sit and I stay.
But I'm never, ever alone.

I jump up and down.
I spin all around.
But I'm never, ever alone.

My Shepherd is there—
He's everywhere,
And that can be written in stone.

Dear God, thank You for
watching over me wherever I go.

Bedtime Treasure

God is a good Father who cares for His children.

What do you think God's family is like?

Dear God, thank You for
being a great Father. Amen.

21

Jesus Loves You

Jesus took the children in his arms. He
put his hands on them and blessed them.
MARK 10:16

Have you ever felt really small or felt like you didn't matter? Maybe you've thought that you'll be more important when you're older. But Jesus said that children are very important. He loves you just the way you are.

Jesus Welcomes the Children

Some children came to see the **Lord**,
But they were shooed away.
Then Jesus said to His **disciples**,
"You must let them stay!

"I'll scoop up all these little ones,
Their **hearts** are pure and true.
If you would like to see My **kingdom**,
Do as children do!"

Jesus welcoming the little
children is from Mark 10.

Little One

Jesus said, "Let the little children come to me."
MATTHEW 19:14

Little one with heart so sweet,
Loved so much from head to feet,
Look at what God's given you—
Moon so white and sky so blue,
Stars that sparkle in the night,
Sun to give each day its light.

Little one with heart so sweet,
Loved so much from head to feet,
Look at how God cares for you,
Every day in all you do.
Sleep now snugly; He is near.
Through the night His love is here.

Dear God, I pray my sleep will be sweet in Your **faithful**, **loving** care.

How did you **trust** God today?

Did He help you in a special way?

Obey and Be Blessed

Listen to your mom and dad.
Do what God says too.
You'll be oh so happy,
And good things will come to you.

GOD'S WORD

Obey your parents in all
things. This pleases the Lord.

COLOSSIANS 3:20

When your parents speak, do you open your ears?
Do you smile and **happily** do what you hear?

God is the best leader to follow.

How do you follow God?

Dear God, help me to obey
You every day. Amen.

24

Help Others

Do not forget to do good to others. And share with them what you have. These are the sacrifices that please God.

HEBREWS 13:16

God wants you to care for other people just as He cares for you! There are so many ways to show you care. If your friends are sad or hurt, you can talk with them and help cheer them up. You can be the happy part of someone's day!

The Good Samaritan

A man was left along the road;
Some thieves had **hurt** him badly.
A priest and Levite passed him by
And did not **help** him, sadly.

But then a good **Samaritan**
Came past and did what's right;
He picked him up and **took** him to
The inn for help that night.

One man showed the **love** of God,
And two went on their way.
If you see **someone** who's been hurt,
Will you help out today?

The story of the Good Samaritan is from Luke 10.

Always Be Helpful

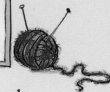

You can use your two small hands
To help someone in need.
Cheer them up with happy words,
Or do a thoughtful deed!

GOD'S WORD

You should do good deeds to be
an example in every way.

TITUS 2:7

Hooray for you if you help someone!
Tell me the **helpful** things you've done!

I pray I'll be brave and **You'll** help me be strong.
I hope in You, God, all day and night long!

Bedtime Treasure

God is with us, so we never have to be afraid.

What are you scared of? Next time you get scared, pray to God and ask for His help.

Dear God, help me to trust in You
so I won't be afraid. Amen.

27

God Is Your Friend

"Now I call you friends."
JOHN 15:15

What makes someone a friend? Good friends are there for you through the good times and bad. They like to play with you and have fun, and they also care when your feelings are hurt or when you are sad. Did you know that God is the greatest friend of all? He never stops caring for you. He wants to be with you every single day!

The Shepherd Comforts

The Lord will hear
your crying, and he
will comfort you.

ISAIAH 30:19

When your heart is sad,
Or maybe even mad,
When you're crying and feeling blue . . .

The Shepherd knows
Just how it goes;
His heart has felt that way too.

So say a prayer—
He's always there
To help and comfort you!

You'll soon feel great—
Just fine, first-rate!
That's what God's love will do!

Dear God, thank You for

being my **friend** when I'm sad.

Good Night, God

Thank You for being **faithful**
and true in all You promise to do.

God Is Faithful to You

"The Lord has great
love and faithfulness."
EXODUS 34:6

Someone who loves you,
Someone who cares,
Someone who's good to you,
Someone who's there . . .

Someone whose promises
Always stand true.
God is a friend who is
Faithful to you!

Bedtime Treasure

God is the best friend there is.

What are your friends like?

Dear God, thank You for being my friend.
Help me to be a good friend to others. Amen.

28

Jesus Gave His Life

"For God loved the world so much that he gave his only Son. God gave his Son so that whoever believes in him may not be lost, but have eternal life."
JOHN 3:16

At the age of thirty-three, Jesus died on the cross. He died so He could take our sins away. But Jesus rose from the grave, and now He lives with God in heaven! And He wants you to live with Him in heaven too. All you have to do to live with Jesus is to be saved. Just believe in Jesus and follow Him, and you can live in heaven someday!

Dear God, thank You for being kind and loving me—even when I make mistakes.

Bedtime Treasure

God's forgiveness makes our hearts clean.

Do you need to ask God for forgiveness today? What for?

Dear God, please forgive me
when I disobey. Amen.

30

God Is with You

The Lord your God will go with you.
He will not leave you or forget you.
DEUTERONOMY 31:6

Did you know that you are never alone? God is always with you! He even knows your fears and worries. But you don't ever have to be afraid if you remember that God is taking care of you. Even when you don't feel good or something bad happens, God will be with you through it all.

The Great Commission

Jesus went up a mountain,
Found in Galilee.
He met with His disciples,
Who hurried there to see.

Jesus told them, "I rule now,
In heaven and on earth.
Teach the world what I've taught *you*,
For this will have great worth!

"I will always be with you,
From now until the end."
Then Jesus rose into the heavens,
Your Savior and your Friend.

Read about the **Great Commission** in
Mark 16, Luke 24, and Matthew 28.

God Is Always with You

"You can be sure that I will
be with you always."
MATTHEW 28:20

A bird will perch to sing a song,
Then quickly fly away . . .
The sun will rise and shine on you,
Then set to end the day.

The dandelions stand and bloom,
Then float off on the breeze . . .
The squirrel will stop to sit up straight,
Then scurry if you sneeze.

But listen closely, little one,
Though most things come and go—
God is *always* where you are.
He loves you head to toe!

Good Night, God

Thank You that I'm never alone.
You are always with me.

Bedtime Treasure

We don't have to be afraid because God is always with us.

What are you worried or sad about? Do you feel better knowing that God is with you?

Dear God, thank You for being with me.
I am so glad You are near. Amen.